IN SEARCH OF
THE SEVEN WONDERS
OF NOAH

*"Also he sent forth the dove from him, to see if
the waters were abated from the face of the
ground; but the dove found no rest for the sole
of her foot, and she returned to him in the ark,
for the waters were on the face of the whole
earth: then he put out his hand, and took her,
and pulled her in to him into the ark. And he
waited yet another seven days; and again he sent
forth the dove out of the ark; and the dove came
in to him in the evening; and, lo, in her mouth
was an olive leaf plucked off: so Noah knew
that the waters were abated from off the earth.
And he waited yet another seven days; and sent
forth the dove; which returned not again to him
any more."*   — GEN. 8 : 8-12

IN SEARCH OF THE SEVEN WONDERS OF NOAH

Daphne M. Cohen, B.A., M.S.
and
Michele Aronoff, B.A.

Illustrations by Katerina Jircik

Treasure Garden Productions, Inc.

International Standard Book Number:
0-9668892-0-7

Library of Congress Catalog Card Number:
98-90962

Design and Pre-press Production
by Matrix Productions Limited
Edited by Dawn Martin
Printed in Canada

Treasure Garden Productions, Inc.
P.O. Box 738
Massapequa Park, NY 11762-0738
U.S.A.

DEDICATIONS

In loving memory of my beloved grandparents: Miriam Landmann, her warm love will forever be in my heart; Aaron and Rachel Cohen *z"l*.   — D. COHEN

In loving memory of my grandpa Max Tusher, who managed to always enlighten me with his stories. In loving memory of my great Aunt Lillian Stein and grandfather Joseph Aronoff *z"l*
                                                        — M. ARONOFF

ACKNOWLEDGMENTS

To my parents Arthur and Nurith Cohen and my grandfather Jonas Landmann who have all inspired me to write this book.

A special thanks to my father, Arthur Cohen, for all his support, not only in writing this book, but in helping me bring this entire project to fruition. His encouragement helped me through many rough times. He taught me to remember that all rainy days come to an end, and that bright sunshine and beautiful rainbows will follow.

To my Great Aunt and Uncle, Bertel and Abush Lewin, on Kibbutz Lavie and to the rest of the family in Israel who encouraged me to pursue my studies in Jerusalem for a year.

I would like to thank the Almighty God for giving me the strength to complete this project.

— D. COHEN

CONTENTS

INTRODUCTION

An Enchanted Treasure Garden

Have you ever taken a long walk and then suddenly realized that you were lost? Well, what I am about to tell you is a special story ... one that is beyond everyone's belief and wildest imagination.

There is an enchanted place called Woody's Treasure Garden and it's located in Eden.

The story begins when six children decide to take a walk through the forest. Ruthy, the youngest, chased a cute fluffy squirrel. Her big brother Josh saw her disappear deep into the forest and immediately ran after her.

Their friends, Sarah, Dena, David, and little Ben followed. They soon realized that they were all lost in the forest.

All of a sudden a beautiful glow of light caught their attention. As they looked closer, they realized that they had reached a magnificent enchanted treasure garden.

The boys ran on ahead but the girls were hesitant to follow. They all gathered in the middle of the treasure garden where they saw four flowers and a big fluffy cloud attached to a beautiful rainbow. A tiny bird perched on top of a tree that sat at the center of the treasure garden.

In her usual habit, Ruthy's curious mind led her away from her brother and their friends. She wandered over to the four flowers and bent down to smell the biggest one.

As Ruthy smelled the flower, she murmured that it smelled very nice. To her surprise, the flower answered Ruthy and said that she always tried to smell her best.

Ruthy screamed and this sent an alarm to all the children that something was wrong. They rushed over to her and asked why she had screamed. Ruthy said that the flower had spoken.

The children laughed because they didn't believe her. They thought she had eaten much too much candy. Josh thought his sister might be telling one of her stories, but at the back of his mind he was wondering where they were.

All of a sudden they all heard a voice. It was a voice that seemed to come from the tree and it was welcoming everyone. Ben ran over to the tree and asked if it had said something.

Sarah interrupted Ben and said that trees can't talk. Just then, the tree spoke again, and said that though it's true trees can't talk, in Woody's Treasure Garden everyone can talk.

All the children were surprised. Ben said to the tree, "Wow, you really can talk. What's your name?" The tree responded by saying that his name was Woody — the Tree of Life.

The children were so excited. Ruthy smiled and shouted out that she had been right all along about the talking flower.

So all of the children ran over to the flowers and overheard the largest flower, the mother, talking to her three children. She was telling them that they must straighten up their leaves and smell their best because they had company.

Ruthy asked the flowers, "What are your names?"

The mother flower answered that her name was Rosy. She told her children to introduce themselves. Rebecca, the oldest, went first followed by Seth and finally Sammy the baby.

Suddenly Debby Bee flew by and introduced herself and told them that she didn't mean to interrupt, but she needed to collect nectar from Rosy because it was beelicious.

Then they heard a strong hissing sound coming from the bushes. Woosh! A slithery creature slid quickly across the ground. "Try to catch me if you can. I'm loose in the garden here to cause trouble for man."

Woody explained, "That was Simon the Snake. He is so sneaky that he was the one who convinced Adam and Eve to eat from the forbidden tree."

Suddenly, a beautiful pink bird flew down from the top of Woody and landed on a low branch. She said that her name was Jenna Bird and she whistled a pretty tune for everyone to hear. After her song was over she flew away and flapped her wings as if to say goodbye.

As she flew away, she passed by Anna Cloud,

who is attached to Lorraine Bow. Both the cloud and the rainbow smiled at the children.

Just then a swirl of wind came from the sky. "It's a plane, no it's a bird, yes and it looks like a dove," shouted Dena. Woody said, "Don't worry. I will make sure you will meet him later." The dove flew by, waving his soft feathery wings.

David ran over to Woody and said, "Wow, there are so many names to remember." Woody chuckled and said that they hadn't met everyone yet.

They still hadn't met Mikey and Mimmy Monkey. Suddenly, they both jumped down from Woody's higher branches. Mikey greeted everyone with a huge smile on his face and his sister waved a big hello.

After Mikey and Mimmy climbed back up the tree, the children heard a voice shouting from the sky high above.

"Woody, you haven't introduced me yet!" Woody shouted back, "Sonny, I could never forget about you. Children, meet Sonny, the sun." The children looked up and waved to Sonny.

Woody realized that there was still someone who the children hadn't met yet, Doobie Bear. Doobie was a great big cuddly brown bear who was always

shy around new people. But Woody convinced Doobie to come out and introduce himself. Then Doobie gave the children a great big hug because he felt very comfortable around them.

Ruthy and little Ben ran over to talk to Lorraine Bow. Ruthy said, "I sure love your beautiful colors." Lorraine Bow answered, "Thank you. If it weren't for all these seven colors bound together then I wouldn't glow so brightly."

Woody agreed and told all of the children that Lorraine Bow was correct. The number seven is a very special number. The children all had a puzzled look on their faces. They wondered why the number seven was so special.

Woody could see that the children didn't understand. So he asked them if they could think of something relating to the number seven.

Ben said, "What about Snow White and the Seven Dwarfs?" Sammy, the youngest flower asked, "Who's that?" All the children laughed. Sarah said, "There are seven days in a week."

Woody agreed and asked if they could think of anything else.

Woody asked if they had ever heard of the Seven Universal Laws of Noah. The children answered that

they had never heard of these laws before. Josh asked if these laws were similar to the Ten Commandments that Moses was given at Mount Sinai.

Woody explained that these Seven Universal Laws were given to Noah, who came before the time of Moses. Woody realized that in order to explain to the children how important these laws were, he must tell them a story.

So he had everyone in the treasure garden gather around to listen as he began his tale.

As the children sat quietly, Woody looked into the eyes of each child. He told them that they were not the first to stumble into the treasure garden.

A long time ago there was a Grandpa named Noah who was walking through the forest with his three grandchildren Rachel, Aaron, and Miriam. They were all talking and asking so many questions that they too got lost and came across my treasure garden by mistake.

I heard Miriam ask, "Grandpa, are you related to that man in the Bible named Noah?" Grandpa answered, "Yes, Noah is the biblical father of all the people in the world after the flood."

Just as I was about to welcome them, Aaron asked his Grandpa a very good question. "Is there a set of rules that everyone in the world can follow to help them get along with each other?" Grandpa Noah said that he wasn't sure.

I decided that it wasn't quite the right time to introduce myself, so as Grandpa Noah and the children turned their heads away from me, I quickly motioned to Doobie Bear to bring me the magic globe.

As Doobie moved the globe out from behind me, I quickly attached a special piece of paper to it, entitled **Helpful Hints**.

Doobie snuck behind the family and gently placed the magic globe on the ground. When they turned around, they were quite surprised to see the sparkling, bright globe in front of them.

Grandpa Noah pulled off the **Helpful Hints** and began to read out loud,

WIN A PRIZE

Search For
The Seven Wonders Of Noah.

9

HELPFUL HINTS

There will be seven clues that will take you on an exciting trip around the world. On each of the seven continents, you will discover another one of the Seven Universal Laws of Noah.

When you come to each place in the world you will see both the good and bad side of the land. First, you will experience the *left* side of the land, where the laws of Noah are not being followed. Then on the *right* side, the land will be glowing as all the people keep the Seven Universal Laws of Noah.

At the end of the voyage, you will see how all the different people in the world can live side by side.

1

Hola! The Search Begins

Grandpa Noah wasn't sure if he should read further, but his grandchildren pushed him to continue.
    He then read,

CLUE #1

Here's your first clue;
This is a special search just for you.
Here's how you can begin.
Do everything right and you can win.
Now you are like detectives
on your first case,
so place your hands on South America
while you count Uno, Dos, Tres.

They all placed their hands on the globe and then there was a flash of lightning and wind swirled around them, followed by a burst of thunder.

Grandpa Noah shouted, "Don't worry kids. It's just a storm." It was not a storm. It was a force so powerful that it picked them all up and as they hung on tightly to the globe, it brought them down to Buenos Aires, Argentina in South America.

They felt they had no choice but to read on in order to finish this journey and return to the treasure garden safely. Grandpa read the **Helpful Hints**.

**Step to the left in order to see
that without law number one
how life might be.**

They all moved their feet to the *left*, and found themselves in a dark, gloomy place.

There were three different groups of people around them. The first group was busy building a statue in the shape of a triangle.

After it was completed, they went down on their hands and knees and started praying to it.

The next group made an even bigger statue. This one's shape was that of a woman's head matched to a cat's body, and it was named Sheba.

The third group built the largest statue of all. It was ten feet high and it looked like they wanted it to reach right up to the sky. This one was a circle shape and red lights beamed out from it. It was scary.

The first group became jealous of the second. They ran over and tried to break the statue. Then all the groups began to fight with each other.

The first group screamed out, "We have the best state, yes we do. We have the best one, but not you."

"No," shouted the second group. "Our statue is number one. Our statue is the most fun."

The third group grew even more angry with the others and screamed, "Our statue is the best of them all. Our statue is the most tall."

Then everyone began to scream at the same time, "We are number one." War broke out among the three groups. Pushing, shouting, screaming — sounds of anger filled the entire land.

Grandpa Noah was afraid for his grandchildren's safety. He quickly read what was next on the **Helpful Hints**. It said,

I know by now you must be in a fright,
so to see life with law number one,
you must step to the right.

They all stepped to the *right*.

This side of the land looked so different. Here, there was harmony and peace. Flowers were blooming everywhere.

Grandpa Noah and his grandchildren saw a magnificent building and decided to go check it out.

Everyone inside was singing. Grandpa Noah asked a man, "What are you all doing?" The man laughed. He said, "We are all praying to the one universal God who is so magnificent."

15

Grandpa Noah explained to his grandchildren, "In the dark gloomy land everyone was so hateful as they all prayed to many different gods, but here everyone is praying to one God."

"Worshipping idols is like making fun of God." Grandpa Noah understood that law number one means **the belief in one God**.

Just then they saw, for just a second, a flash of red light. Seeing it was a pure delight. It was a beautiful and breathtaking sight.

Grandpa Noah and the children knew that they must find out the rest of the clues in order to return to the treasure garden.

2

An Adventure to the Land Down Under

It was time to continue on their journey. Grandpa Noah took out the **Helpful Hints** to see what came next.

CLUE #2

In order to learn clue number two
put your hands on Australia,
that's what you should do.

They picked up the magic globe and placed their hands on the continent of Australia.

Just like before, there was a flash of lightning, and swirling winds around them, followed by a burst of thunder. The next thing they knew they were in Sydney, Australia. They read on,

Now it's time for you to see,
without law number two,
how life would be.
Sadly, again you must step to the left
to see how poorly this land is kept.

Just as they stepped to the *left* they heard loud shouts of anger. They saw two women arguing. Each of them had their sons standing with them.

Suddenly, one woman started screaming and saying bad words to the other woman. Then they were both shouting and cursing at each other.

Grandpa Noah tried to cover his grandchildren's ears.

In the meantime, the two sons standing with their mothers started fighting with each other as well. They were all screaming at one another because they were so angry.

One of the women got so mad that she started cursing at God. Grandpa Noah and the kids were getting so upset that they said it was time to take out their **Helpful Hints** and read on.

Seeing this argument is a terrible sight.
To see how important law number two is,
take a step to the right.

To their surprise, they saw the same two women with their sons.

Grandpa Noah looked at the **Helpful Hints** to see if they had followed the instructions correctly.

Miriam tapped Grandpa Noah on the arm in order to get his attention. He looked up and couldn't believe his eyes.

The same two women who had been arguing suddenly started laughing. They realized how silly their argument was and how foolish it was for them to get so upset.

"We should be thankful for everything that we have in this world," agreed both women and their sons.

Grandpa Noah told the kids, "When we stepped to the *left* we saw the two women who were so mad at each other that they became angry with God. Then, when we stepped to the *right*, we saw them together as friends and thanking God for everything, therefore law number two is that **we shouldn't curse God**."

Just then a flash of red and orange light came across Grandpa Noah and the children's eyes. It was a wonderful surprise. The colors were so prettily blended together that a happy feeling grew inside them all. They were really starting to have a ball. Red and orange were so neat, but everything was not yet complete.

3

Journey Through a
Hole to China

They all knew it was time to continue on with their adventure. Aaron read from the **Helpful Hints** this time.

CLUE #3
In order to learn clue number three, touch the continent Asia and hold on as tight as can be.

A huge hole opened up in the ground directly below them. Aaron screamed out, "Oh no! This is why we should hold on tight!"

They all fell into the hole. Rachel and Miriam started to scream.

"What's happening to us?" they all shouted, as they all hung on as tight as they could.

While they were traveling through the hole, Grandpa Noah thought of the two clues they had figured out so far. He wondered what law number three was going to be.

Finally, they saw an opening at the far end of the hole. They reached the end and the next thing everyone knew, they were falling from the sky.

Just then a large dove flew near to them and

seemed to want to help. The dove stretched out his giant wings and he swooped down under them all. Grandpa Noah and the children landed on the dove's soft, feathery wings.

The dove flew slowly to the ground and dropped them off gently. Before they even had a chance to thank the dove, he was on his way.

Rachel saw a sign that read, "Welcome to Hong Kong, China."

Miriam took out the **Helpful Hints** for clue number three.

Step to the left and you will see
how the world is without
law number three.

Everyone was afraid but they knew that they must go on. As they stepped to the *left*, they all felt a cold shivery feeling go up their spines.

They found themselves on the bank of a river, watching a boat sailing by. On board the boat, there was a Captain and a fisherman.

At first, they seemed as though they were just talking, but Grandpa Noah realized that the two men were really arguing.

23

"Oh no! Not another fight," cried Miriam.

The men were fighting over the direction in which to steer the boat. The Captain wanted to steer the boat in the opposite direction to where the fisherman wanted to go because he thought the winds were too strong.

Finally, the Captain pushed the fisherman so hard that he fell into the river. The waves were so rough that it was hard for the fisherman to swim.

The fisherman screamed for help. There were tears of fear running down his face. "Somebody please help me," he shouted.

Grandpa Noah was so upset that he wanted to jump into the water to save him. Just as he was about to dive in, his terrified grandchildren pushed him to the *right*, without even looking at the **Helpful Hints**.

They all found themselves on a canoe, floating down the river. When Aaron looked around he saw that the fisherman was still drowning.

Grandpa Noah paddled through the waves and screamed out to the fisherman, "Grab on to this paddle and I will pull you in."

The fisherman held on to the paddle with all of his might while Grandpa Noah and the children pulled him up.

Just then they heard another voice screaming from far away. "Help me, the winds are too strong for me to steer my boat," cried the Captain.

"Grandpa, we have to help him, otherwise his boat might turn over," shouted Rachel.

"Please help me," cried the Captain.

"Look over there," screamed Rachel, "he has fallen overboard."

Miriam said, "He must have been caught in the strong, stormy winds. That's why he got thrown out of his boat."

"Don't worry, Grandpa Noah and the gang are here to save you," shouted Aaron.

As Grandpa Noah paddled furiously towards the Captain he screamed, "Hold on real tight to the paddle while we pull you in."

"How can I ever thank you for saving my life?" asked the Captain. Grandpa Noah asked, "Do you understand why it was wrong for you to push the fisherman and cause him to fall into the river?"

"How could I have been so mean? If you hadn't saved him, the fisherman could have drowned. I will never again leave someone when they are in trouble because I sure know how it feels. Thank you for all your help," said the Captain.

Grandpa Noah explained to his grandchildren why law number three was so important **to respect human life**.

Just then a flash of red, orange, and yellow light was shining upon their faces. These three colors were as pretty as lace and made them feel right in place. It was so breathtaking and beautiful for them to see; a warmth filled their hearts as they saw those three.

4

In the Land of Liberty

Now that the group understood the first three laws, it was time for them to continue on their exciting journey.

Rachel pulled out the **Helpful Hints** to read clue number four:

CLUE #4
**Put your hands on
the continent of North America
so you can learn some more.
Place your hands right now
and learn law number four.**

**Look up and see the dove again fly,
and he will take you into the sky,
where you can learn the importance
of law number four and why.**

As they approached the golden land of America, they saw the Statue of Liberty waving her torch high in the sky.

"I can't believe it. We are in the Big Apple — New York," screamed Rachel.

Miriam wandered away from her family in order to find out what was on the *left* side. She heard a little girl crying. She found the crying girl, sitting in front of her house.

She went over to the girl and asked, "What's wrong? Why are you so upset?"

"My parents got into a big fight," the child cried.

Meanwhile, Grandpa Noah had noticed that Miriam was missing. He began to look for her. An hour passed and there was still no sign of Miriam anywhere.

They saw that the Helpful Hints were missing and realized that she must have taken it. "Miriam must have gone to the *left*. She is impatient and has always tried to get the things she didn't like over with, like her homework," cried Rachel. Aaron said, "That's the total opposite of me." All at once they stepped to the *left* in order to find Miriam.

Rachel saw Miriam talking to a little girl. Grandpa Noah shouted, "We all got scared when we couldn't find you, Miriam.

"You should never have taken off like that without telling us where you were going."

"I am very sorry. Everything was happening so quickly," answered Miriam.

Just as Grandpa Noah approached Miriam they all heard shouting coming from within the house. "What's going on in there?" asked Rachel.

"It's my parents screaming at each other. They have been fighting all day."

"What's your name?" asked Grandpa Noah. "My name is Lillian," she answered.

Just then a loud thump came from inside the house. Then a bang! "I think we should see what's going on in there. What are your parents' names?" asked Grandpa Noah.

"Nina and Joseph Smith," she whispered. Bam! Boom! The noise in the house grew louder, with more terrible sounds.

"I can't listen to this anymore," cried Lillian as she ran off. Miriam started to run after her.

Grandpa Noah shouted, "Come back, Miriam. We will meet up with her later." Miriam reluctantly rejoined the gang.

Grandpa Noah felt that he should speak with Lillian's parents. He rang the doorbell.

A man's voice shouted, "Well, don't just stand there. Why don't you get the door?" A woman screamed back, "What do you think I am doing, Joseph?"

A woman with an angry face and tears rolling down her cheeks opened the door. "What do you want?" asked the woman.

Grandpa Noah explained to her how he had seen their daughter crying outside, and she had run away because she was so upset.

"I think you better come listen to this, Joseph," Nina shouted out to her husband. The look of anger on both their faces turned to fear.

They asked Grandpa Noah what he thought they should do. He said, "Don't worry. Follow me and we shall see." They left the house and stepped to the *right*.

They found themselves in front of a house that looked just like Lillian's but this one belonged to a little girl named Judy. The difference between this house and Lillian's was that sounds of laughter were coming from within.

"Judy Parker is one of Lillian's best friends. She is probably there," explained Mrs. Smith.

Anxiously, they went to the door. Mrs. Smith rang the doorbell. Mrs. Parker warmly invited them in.

Lillian's mother asked if her daughter was there. Mrs. Parker smiled and told them what a wonderful

time Lillian was having. "You have such a nice daughter. She was a little upset when she first arrived, but it didn't take her long to cheer up," said Mrs. Parker.

Just then Mr. Parker came into the living room to greet his guests. The Smiths started to explain why Lillian was so upset.

The Parkers then explained how important family values are. "This is our secret to such a happy household," said Mrs. Parker. "We always communicate with each other and try to work out our problems."

"This is much better than fighting and getting upset which could lead to a break-up of a happy family," explained Mr. Parker.

Just then Lillian and Judy came running down the stairs to see who had come to visit. Lillian was happy to see Grandpa Noah and the gang again.

Lillian's parents explained to her that they now realized how much they upset her and they would love for her to come home with them.

"The Parkers have shown us how important family values are," said Mrs. Smith. Lillian was happy to hear all of this.

"I think that our time here is up, kids," said Grandpa Noah. Lillian gave them all a great big hug goodbye.

Once outside, a very confused look came over Rachel's face. She didn't quite understand law number four.

Grandpa Noah explained that when they were on the *left* side they saw an angry family, but on the *right*, there was a very happy family. Grandpa Noah said, "**husbands and wives should love and respect each other and we have to value the family.**"

Just then they all saw four colors flash before them. They were all so shiny like a gem. They were red, orange, yellow, and green. These beautiful colors looked fit for a queen.

5

A Visit to the
Home of the Penguins

Aaron wanted to announce the next clue from the **Helpful Hints**.

CLUE #5

Hold on to the continent Antarctica because now it's time for you to dive into learning law number five.

Just as before, there was thunder, lightning and swirls of wind. Luckily, they found themselves

dressed in warm coats, scarves, and hats as they realized that they were down near the South Pole.

They were all freezing and shivering. They had landed in the coldest part of Antarctica, and then without realizing it, they all stepped to the *left*.

A boat came into view and then seven men came ashore. There were penguins everywhere and Aaron couldn't get over how cute they looked.

Just then Aaron noticed that the men were gathering the penguins together. "What are those men doing with all of those penguins?" asked Aaron. Grandpa Noah didn't like the looks of it.

Aaron ran over to the men to find out what was going on. "What do you think you are doing with all of those penguins?" he asked.

The men explained that they were tourists and they wanted to bring these animals back to their country for pets.

"That isn't a very good idea," cried Rachel.

The men just looked at her and laughed. They took the penguins and went back on to their boat.

Aaron was upset to hear the penguins whimpering. "We have to hurry and stop them before they get away," shouted Miriam.

Quickly, Grandpa Noah and the gang jumped onto their boat in order to chase after them.

Grandpa Noah screamed out, "If you steal the penguins away from here they might not be able to survive."

Just then, the men steered their ship to the *right*, and then all of a sudden they saw the light. All seven men turned pale.

They now understood it wasn't right for them to steal. They knew it was wrong, so they turned around and let all the penguins go.

The children all agreed that law number five was easy to understand. "Therefore law number five is **not to steal**," said Rachel.

"By the way, stealing was one reason that in the biblical story of Noah there was a great big flood," explained Grandpa Noah.

All of a sudden they saw beautiful colors. They were red, orange, yellow, green and blue. These colors blended together just like glue. Continue on with their journey, that's what they must do.

6

Travel to the
Land of Royalty

Miriam took out the **Helpful Hints** and read on for clue number six.

CLUE #SIX

It's time to learn law number six.
I promise you that
you will get your kicks.
Touch the continent of Europe
and you will be,
in the land of royalty.

They found to their surprise, they were sitting on the top deck of a tour bus in London, England.

"On our *left* side, we are approaching the Palace and we are just in time to see the Changing of the Guard," announced the tour guide.

"Can we get any closer? It's so difficult to see," shouted Rachel. All the kids on the bus started to scream, "Move the bus closer, we can't see."

Just then the bus driver lost control of the bus and they went crashing into the left side of the Palace gate. A loud scream came from within the Palace. Luckily no one was hurt, but the gate was destroyed.

Security guards rushed to the scene of the accident. People came running out of the palace to see what had happened.

One of the guards was so angry with the bus driver that he started to scream at him. "You must pay for all the damage that you did," shouted the guard.

Grandpa Noah agreed that the argument needed to be settled, but not in that way.

On the *right* side of the street there was a courthouse. Grandpa Noah knew this was where they must go in order to settle their argument.

Both the guard and the bus driver presented their cases to the Judge. The court announced that the bus driver needed to pay a fine for the damage to the gate.

The kids were so excited that they understood law number six which is that *we have to set up courts of justice*.

"This is the best way to solve problems and that way everything is fair," said Miriam. Grandpa Noah explained that courts are set up to bring justice to the world.

Then they saw the colors red, orange, yellow, green, blue and indigo. The colors certainly did glow. They knew they had one more law to go.

7

On Safari in Africa

Rachel read from the **Helpful Hints**:

CLUE #7
It's time to visit another land.
On Africa you must place your hands.

The next thing they knew they were on safari in Kenya, Africa.

"Look to your *left* and you will see some lions, elephants, zebras and monkeys," announced the tour guide.

43

Rachel couldn't believe her eyes. She saw a lion trying to eat a zebra while the zebra was still walking around. "Oh! I can't bear to watch," she screamed.

"I think that's so cool," said a little boy sitting right in front of them.

"How can you say that?" shouted Aaron.

"The lion must be really hungry, so why should he have to wait until his prey is dead to eat his dinner? He likes to just dive right in," giggled the boy.

"That is being so cruel to animals," answered Miriam.

"Hang on tight. We are going to take a quick turn to the *right*," announced the tour guide. On the right side they saw the same lion again trying to eat the zebra.

"Let's try to scare the lion away with our jeep," cried Aaron. "O.K. that could be fun too," the little boy said.

"Hang on kids, here we go," shouted the tour guide. Zoom! Zoom! The lion ran away. "That really scared him off. I don't think he will be coming back any time soon," said Aaron.

"What did all of this have to do with the laws of Noah?" asked Miriam.

Aaron answered, "Well the Noahide Laws apply only to the world of human beings, and *people should have respect for living animals*. We should only eat from an animal that has been killed first.

"You mean we shouldn't do what the lion was about to do with the zebra?" asked the little boy.

"That's right," answered Grandpa Noah.

All of a sudden they saw the colors red, orange, yellow, and green. Beautiful as they have ever been seen. Blue, indigo, and violet. They knew this adventure they would never forget. They all jumped up high and tried to reach the sky.

They couldn't believe that they were done. They finished the laws one by one and had so much fun.

"Hooray!" they shouted, "We make a great team." It was time for them to go back to the treasure garden that was full of gleam.

CONCLUSION

The Seven Universal Laws of Noah

As they looked up at the rainbow they saw something flying towards them. It was the same dove that had helped them before. He landed and spread out his wings.

They had no idea what they were supposed to do next. They took one last look at the **Helpful Hints** and read,

Now you must climb aboard the dove.
He will protect you like a glove.

They all sat down on the wings of the dove and flew off into the rainbow.

"Well kids, that's the whole story," announced Woody.

Ben said, "Well, then what happened?"

Dena asked, "Did they meet everyone in the treasure garden like we did?"

Woody chuckled and replied "Well no, not yet." The children couldn't understand what Woody meant.

Just then all the kids looked up at the sky and saw a dove fly out from Lorraine Bow. As the dove landed, Grandpa Noah, Aaron, Rachel and Miriam slid off his wings.

The children in the treasure garden were surprised to see them. Sarah asked Woody, "Why did you say that this happened a long time ago?"

Woody answered, "When someone travels through the magic globe it takes a very long time."

Grandpa Noah and the gang stood with their mouths wide open, since they had never before seen a talking tree.

Woody finally introduced himself and explained to them why it had been so important for them to go on this journey.

David ran over to Woody and told him why the number seven is so special. "A rainbow needs all of its seven colors to glow. If just one color was missing, it would not be complete," said David.

Aaron explained, "The same thing goes for all the laws of Noah. We need each and every one of them."

"How would you like to tell everyone what these Seven Laws are?" asked Grandpa Noah.

Aaron answered, "I would love to." And so he began.

THE SEVEN UNIVERSAL LAWS OF NOAH

LAW ONE:

Belief in one God.

LAW TWO:

Do not curse God.

LAW THREE:

Respect human life.

LAW FOUR:

Respect the family.

LAW FIVE:

Do not steal.

LAW SIX:

Set up courts of justice.

LAW SEVEN:

Respect living animals.

Woody winked at Aaron. Rachel asked Woody, "Are we going to get a prize now?"

Grandpa Noah interrupted Rachel and said "I believe learning the Seven Universal Laws of Noah is the reward." Woody smiled at Grandpa Noah.

Ruthy ran over to the dove to find out his name. "My name is Jonah and I symbolize universal peace," whistled the dove. Everyone in the treasure garden began to sing and dance.

Finally, Sonny started to yawn because it was almost time for him to set. It was getting late and all the children realized it was time for them to go home.

Jonah offered everyone a ride home on his wings. Woody smiled and told them all to come and visit his treasure garden again real soon.

THE END

WOODY'S TREASURE GARDEN

There is no other place in the world quite like it.

It is a magical place, beyond everyone's belief and wildest imagination, where anyone and everyone is welcome.

One day, you too may stumble into the treasure garden for a fun visit with Woody and all his pals.

ABOUT THE AUTHORS

Daphne M. Cohen holds a Master of Science degree in Jewish Education from Yeshiva University and a Bachelor of Arts degree in Elementary Education and Judaic Studies from Touro College. For a full academic year she studied at Neve Yerushalayim College in Jerusalem, Israel. Currently, Daphne is completing her Graduate Certificate in Judaica Librarianship from Gratz College.

Her extensive teaching background is in religious schools and libraries. In addition, Ms. Cohen is President and Curriculum Consultant of Treasure Garden Productions, Inc. and is also the author of children's books. Daphne is a recipient of the Gela, Leon and Michael Maneli Foundation Fellowship from Yeshiva University and the Doris Orenstein Memorial Fund Award from the Association of Jewish Libraries. Currently, she is a member of the Association of Children's Book Writers and Illustrators, the Association of Jewish Book Publishers, the Coalition for the Advancement of Jewish Education and the Association of Jewish Libraries.

Michele Aronoff holds a Bachelor of Arts degree in Psychology and Communications from Touro College. She is currently undergoing a Master's program in Special Education at New York University. She has written two articles for the Jewish Press titled *My Grandfather* and *A Titanic Lesson*. Currently, Michele is an author of children's books.

ABOUT THE ILLUSTRATOR

Katerina Jircik is a Canadian artist, with a very creative family background. She has studied both in Canada and at Tulane University. In addition to her work as an illustrator, Katerina also creates mixed media artwork, using wood, paper and fabrics, which she shows and sells in local art galleries.

Treasure Garden Productions, Inc.

P.O. Box 738
Massapequa Park, NY
11762-0738
U.S.A.

Telephone and Fax:
(516) 541-7173
e-mail:
daphne@treasuregardenet.com

If you have enjoyed *In Search of the Seven Wonders of Noah* and would like to order more copies, please complete the form below.
    Both parents and educators might like to purchase the companion Resource Manual, priced $12.95. This booklet is full of background material and creative activities which are specifically based on this book.

In Search of the Seven Wonders of Noah

☐ Book and Resource Manual   **$19.95**
(if purchased together)

☐ Book only   **$9.95**

☐ Resource Manual   **$12.95**

Add $3.00 for shipping and handling for US orders.

New York State residents please add 8.5% Sales Tax
(Book & Manual $1.69; Book 85¢; Manual $1.10)
International Orders should request estimate of shipping costs.

Enclose Check or Money Order payable in US Dollars
to Treasure Garden Productions, Inc. totaling: $. . . . .

Name: . . . .

Address: . . . .

City . . . . State/Prov. . . . .

Country . . . . Zip/Postal Code . . . .

"And God said, This is the token of the covenant which I make between me and you and every living creature that is with you, for perpetual generations: I have set my bow in the cloud, and it shall be for a token of a covenant between me and the earth."   — GEN. 9 : 12-13